Asian Soup Cookbook

A Collection of Easy, Simple and Delicious Asian Soups

By
BookSumo Press

Published by
http://www.booksumo.com

ENJOY THE RECIPES?
KEEP ON COOKING
WITH 6 MORE FREE
COOKBOOKS!

Click the link below and simply enter your email address
to join the club and receive your 6 cookbooks.

http://booksumo.com/magnet

LEGAL NOTES

Table of Contents

5 . . . . Tofu Mushroom Soup

6 . . . . Udon Soup

7 . . . . Onion Soup

8 . . . . Tofu and Miso

9 . . . . Jap Chae: (Korean Glass Noodles)

10 . . . . . . Seaweed Soup

11 . . . . . . Kimchee Jigeh: (Stew)

12 . . . . . . Miso: (Bean Curd Soup)

13 . . . . . . Doenjang Chigae: (Bean Tofu Soup)

14 . . . . . . Pine Nut Rice Soup

15 . . . . . . Shrimp Rice Soup

16 . . . . . . Seaweed Soup II

17 . . . . . . Tak Toritang: (Potato and Chicken)

18 . . . . . . Soon Du Bu Jigae: (Tofu Stew)

19 . . . . . . Korean Curry

20 . . . . . . Chicken Stew

21 . . . . . . Filipino Oxtail Stew

22 . . . . . . Salmon Stew: (Abalos Style)

23 . . . . . . Picadillo Filipino: (Hamburger Soup)

24 . . . . . . Fish Sinigang: (Tilapia)

25 . . . . . . Sinigang Na Baka: (Beef Soup)

26 . . . . . . Filipino Chicken Stew

27 . . . . . . Tofu Soup

28 . . . . . . Yuan's Favorite Soup

29 . . . . . . Taiwanese Corn Soup

30 . . . . . . Easy Egg and Pea Soup

31 . . . . . . Asian Corn Soup Cream Style

32 . . . . . . Bamboo Rice Soup

33 . . . . . . Potato Soup

34 . . . . . . Suan La Dofu Tang: (Tofu Soup)

35 . . . . . . Hot and Spicy Soup

36 . . . . . . Chi Tan T'ang: (Egg Drop Soup)

37 . . . . . . Cabbage Soup

38 . . . . . . Sweet and Spicy Tofu Soup

39 . . . . . . Easy Wonton Soup

40 . . . . . . Alternative Egg Drop Soup

41 . . . . . . Chinese Melon Soup

42 . . . . . . Natural Ramen Noodles

43 . . . . . . New Classical Ramen

44 . . . . . . Ramen Re-Imagined

45 . . . . . . Super Easy Coconut Soup Thai-Style

46 . . . . . . Simple Cumber Soup with Thai Roots

47 . . . . . . Charong's Favorite Thai Soup of Ginger

48 . . . . . . A Thai Soup of Veggies

49 . . . . . . Easy Coconut Soup

50 . . . . . . Spicy Kale and Onion Soup

51 . . . . . . Lemony Soy Sauce Soup

52 . . . . . . Japanese Mushroom Soup I: (Beef, Cheddar)

53 . . . . . . Japanese Mushroom Soup II: (Miso & Tofu)

Tofu
Mushroom Soup

🥣 Prep Time: 10 mins
🕐 Total Time: 20 mins

Servings per Recipe: 2	
Calories	100 kcal
Carbohydrates	4.8 g
Cholesterol	3 mg
Fat	3.9 g
Fiber	1 g
Protein	11 g
Sodium	1326 mg

Ingredients

3 cups prepared dashi stock
1/4 cup sliced shiitake mushrooms
1 tbsp miso paste
1 tbsp soy sauce
1/8 cup cubed soft tofu
1 green onion, diced

Directions

1. Get a saucepan. Add your stock, get it boiling. Once boiling add mushrooms and cook for 4 mins.
2. Get a bowl. Combine soy sauce and miso paste evenly. Mix this with your stock.
3. For 6 mins let broth cook. Add some diced green onion.
4. Enjoy.

UDON
Soup

Prep Time: 15 mins

Total Time: 40 mins

Servings per Recipe: 4
Calories	548 kcal
Carbohydrates	53.4 g
Cholesterol	206 mg
Fat	17.2 g
Fiber	2.8 g
Protein	42.2 g
Sodium	2491 mg

Ingredients

6 cups prepared dashi stock
1/4 pound chicken, cut into chunks
2 carrots, diced
1/3 cup soy sauce
3 tbsps mirin
1/2 tsp white sugar
1/3 tsp salt
2 (12 ounce) packages firm tofu, cubed
1/3 pound shiitake mushrooms, sliced

5 ribs and leaves of bok choy, diced
1 (9 ounce) package fresh udon noodles
4 eggs
2 leeks, diced

Directions

1. Get a sauce pan. Heat the following: salt, dashi stock, sugar, carrots, mirin, chicken, and soy sauce. Allow everything to lightly boil until your chicken is cooked fully (8 mins).

2. Mix in some bok choy, mushrooms, and tofu. Let everything continue simmering for 6 mins.

3. Add your noodles and cook for 5 more mins. Finally add leeks.

4. Take your eggs and crack them over the soup. Let the soup cook for 5 mins until eggs are done.

5. Enjoy.

Onion
Soup

Prep Time: 15 mins
Total Time: 1 hr

Servings per Recipe: 6

Calories	25 kcal
Carbohydrates	4.4 g
Cholesterol	1 mg
Fat	0.2 g
Fiber	0.9 g
Protein	1.4 g
Sodium	257 mg

Ingredients

1/2 stalk celery, diced
1 small onion, diced
1/2 carrot, diced
1 tsp grated fresh ginger root
1/4 tsp minced fresh garlic
2 tbsps chicken stock
3 tsps beef bouillon granules

1 cup chopped fresh shiitake mushrooms
2 quarts water
1 cup baby Portobello mushrooms, sliced
1 tbsp minced fresh chives

Directions

1. Get a saucepan with high heat. Get the following items boiling before continuing: water, celery, beef bouillon, onion, chicken stock, carrots, half of the mushrooms, ginger, and garlic.
2. Put a lid on the boiling contents. Set heat to a medium level. Let the contents lightly boil for 45 mins.
3. Get another saucepan. Put the other half of mushrooms in it. Once the first pot has been cooking for 45 mins. Strain soup into the pot with uncooked mushrooms.
4. Throw away anything left from the straining.
5. Garnish with chives when served.
6. Enjoy.

TOFU
and Miso

🍲 Prep Time: 15 mins

🕐 Total Time: 17 mins

Servings per Recipe: 6	
Calories	82 kcal
Carbohydrates	4.6 g
Cholesterol	6 mg
Fat	4.5 g
Fiber	0.9 g
Protein	7.4 g
Sodium	358 mg

Ingredients

2 tbsps sesame seeds
1/2 cup dried Asian-style whole sardines
2 1/2 tbsps red miso paste
1/2 cup boiling water
1 (16 ounce) package silken tofu, cubed
4 green onions, thinly sliced
crushed red pepper flakes

Directions

1. Get a skillet and fry sesame seeds until aromatic for 3 mins.
2. Get a pan and begin to boil water.
3. Get a food processor and combine dried sardines and sesame seeds. Process into a powder.
4. Put sesame and sardines in a bowl and combine miso. Combine in your boiling water (1/2 cup) from earlier and mix until creamy.
5. Finally combine your tofu red pepper, and green onions.
6. Enjoy.

Jap Chae
(Korean Glass Noodles)

🥣 Prep Time: 15 mins

🕐 Total Time: 20 mins

Servings per Recipe: 4
Calories	363 kcal
Carbohydrates	65.2 g
Cholesterol	0 mg
Fat	10.7 g
Fiber	0.6 g
Protein	1.9 g
Sodium	1073 mg

Ingredients
1 pkg. (8 serving size) sweet potato vermicelli
half cup reduced-sodium soy sauce
1/4 cup brown sugar
half cup boiling water
three tbsps. vegetable oil
1 tsp. toasted sesame seeds

Directions
1. Cover the vermicelli with hot water after cutting it into small pieces for 10 minutes and add a mixture of soy sauce, boiling water, and brown sugar into it.
2. Cook this mixture in hot oil for about 5 minutes and just before serving, add noodles over it.

SEAWEED
Soup

🥣 Prep Time: 15 mins

🕐 Total Time: 45 mins

Servings per Recipe: 4	
Calories	65 kcal
Carbohydrates	1 g
Cholesterol	17 mg
Fat	3.7 g
Fiber	0.1 g
Protein	6.8 g
Sodium	940 mg

Ingredients
1 (1 ounce) package dried brown seaweed
1/4 lb. beef top sirloin, minced
2 tsps. sesame oil
1 half tbsps. soy sauce
1 tsp. salt, or to taste
6 cups water
1 tsp. minced garlic

Directions
1. Cover seaweed with water to get them soft and cut them into 2 inch pieces.
2. Cook beef, half tbsp. of soy sauce and some salt for about 1 minute in a saucepan over medium heat.
3. Now add seaweed and the remaining soy sauce and cook for another minute while stirring continuously.
4. Bring to boil after adding 2 cups of water and add garlic and the remaining water.
5. Cook this for 20 minutes and add salt before serving.

Kimchee Jigeh (Stew)

Prep Time: 5 mins
Total Time: 25 mins

Servings per Recipe: 4	
Calories	303 kcal
Carbohydrates	10.6 g
Cholesterol	59 mg
Fat	24.1 g
Fiber	3.5 g
Protein	13.7 g
Sodium	2064 mg

Ingredients

6 cups water
three cups napa cabbage Kim Chee, brine reserved
2 cups cubed fully cooked luncheon meat (e.g. Turkey Spam)
three tbsps. chili powder
salt, to taste
ground black pepper, to taste

Directions

1. Take a large saucepan and combine water, kim chee, spam, pepper, chili powder, kim chee brine and salt.
2. Bring this mixture to boil and cook for about 20 minutes.
3. Serve.

MISO
(Bean Curd Soup)

Prep Time: 15 mins

Total Time: 35 mins

Servings per Recipe: 4
Calories	158 kcal
Carbohydrates	21.6 g
Cholesterol	0 mg
Fat	4.1 g
Fiber	3.4 g
Protein	9.1 g
Sodium	641 mg

Ingredients
three half cups water
three tbsps. denjang (Korean bean curd paste)
1 tbsp. garlic paste
half tbsp. dashi granules
half tbsp. gochujang (Korean hot pepper paste)
1 zucchini, cubed
1 potato, peeled and cubed
1/4 lb. fresh mushrooms, quartered
1 onion, chopped

1 (12 ounce) package soft tofu, sliced

Directions
1. Combine water, denjang, garlic paste, dashi and gochujang in saucepan over medium heat and let it boil for 2 minutes.
2. Now add zucchini, potato, onions and mushrooms, and cook for another 7 minutes.
3. Now add tofu and cook until tender.

Doenjang Chigae (Bean Tofu Soup)

🥣 Prep Time: 15 mins
🕐 Total Time: 40 mins

Servings per Recipe: 6	
Calories	59 kcal
Carbohydrates	5 g
Cholesterol	0 mg
Fat	2.7 g
Fiber	1.6 g
Protein	4.9 g
Sodium	378 mg

Ingredients

three cups vegetable stock
three cups water
2 cloves garlic, coarsely chopped
2 tbsps. Korean soy bean paste (doenjang)
4 green onions, chopped
1 zucchini, halved and cut into 1/2-inch slices
half (16 ounce) package firm tofu, drained and cubed

1 jalapeno pepper, sliced

Directions

1. Add garlic and soy bean paste into boiled vegetable stock stirring regularly to dissolve.

2. Now add green onion, tofu, jalapeno and zucchini, and cook for 15 minutes at low heat.

3. Serve.

PINE NUT
Rice Soup

Prep Time: 10 mins
Total Time: 20 mins

Servings per Recipe: 6

Calories	275 kcal
Carbohydrates	37 g
Cholesterol	0 mg
Fat	12.5 g
Fiber	3.3 g
Protein	7.8 g
Sodium	2 mg

Ingredients
1 cup pine nuts
2 cups cooked long-grain white rice
6 cups water
1 tbsp. pine nuts
1 cup dates, pitted and chopped
half tsp. white sugar
salt to taste

Directions
1. Blend rice, 1 cup pine nuts, and 2 glass of water in a blender.
2. Add 4 cups of water and this pine nut mixture into saucepan, and bring it to boil.
3. Cook for 10 minutes at low heat while stirring regularly to prevent it from burning.
4. Garnish with sliced dates and more pine nuts.
5. Serve.

Shrimp
Rice Soup

🥣 Prep Time: 2 hrs
🕐 Total Time: 2 hr 20 mins

Servings per Recipe: 4	
Calories	586 kcal
Carbohydrates	99.6 g
Cholesterol	128 mg
Fat	6.8 g
Fiber	1.6 g
Protein	25.9 g
Sodium	131 mg

Ingredients

2 cups white rice
9 ounces shelled and deveined shrimp
1 tbsp. sesame oil
1 tbsp. rice wine
12 cups water
salt to taste

Directions

1. Let the rice stand for about 2 hours after rinsing it.
2. Fry shrimp and rice wine in hot oil in a saucepan over medium heat and add rice cook for 1 minute.
3. Pour some water into the saucepan and when the mixture is thick, turn the heat down to low and cook for another 10 - 15 minutes.
4. Serve.

SEAWEED
Soup II

🥣 Prep Time: 10 mins
🕐 Total Time: 40 mins

Servings per Recipe: 4
Calories   376 kcal
Carbohydrates   21.4 g
Cholesterol   69 mg
Fat   21.9 g
Fiber   0.8 g
Protein   20.6 g
Sodium   1249 mg

Ingredients
1 ounce dried wakame (brown) seaweed
2 tsps. sesame oil
half cup extra-lean ground beef
1 tsp. salt, or to taste
1 half tbsps. soy sauce
1 tsp. minced garlic
7 cups water

Directions
1. Let the seaweed stand in water for about 15 minutes to get soft, drain the water, and cut it into 2 inch pieces.
2. Cook beef, 1/3 cup soy sauce and add some salt in hot oil in a saucepan over medium heat for about 4 minutes and add seaweed and the soy sauce that is left.
3. Cook for another minute and add garlic and some water.
4. Bring water to boil and lower the heat down to low and cook for another 15 minutes.
5. Serve.

Tak
Toritang
(Potato and Chicken)

🥘 Prep Time: 15 mins
🕐 Total Time: 1 hr

Servings per Recipe: 4

Calories	447 kcal
Fat	14.1 g
Carbohydrates	54.7g
Protein	25.7 g
Cholesterol	60 mg
Sodium	1994 mg

Ingredients

2 1/2 lbs chicken drumettes
2 large potatoes, cut into large chunks
2 carrots, cut into 2 inch pieces
1 large onion, cut into 8 pieces
4 cloves garlic, crushed
1/4 C. water
1/2 C. soy sauce

2 tbsps white sugar
3 tbsps hot pepper paste

Directions

1. Get the following boiling in a big pot: hot pepper paste, potatoes, sugar, carrots, soy sauce, water, onions, and garlic.
2. Once it is all boiling set the heat to its lowest level and cook the mix for 50 mins.
3. At this point the liquid should be thick.
4. Enjoy.

SOON
Du Bu Jigae (Tofu Stew)

🥣 Prep Time: 5 mins
🕐 Total Time: 20 mins

Servings per Recipe: 2
Calories   242 kcal
Fat   16.5 g
Carbohydrates   7g
Protein   20 g
Cholesterol   99 mg
Sodium   415 mg

Ingredients
1 tsp vegetable oil
1 tsp Korean chile powder
2 tbsps ground beef (optional)
1 tbsp Korean soy bean paste (doenjang)
1 C. water
salt and pepper to taste
1 (12 oz.) package Korean soon tofu or soft tofu, drained and sliced
1 egg

1 tsp sesame seeds
1 green onion, diced

Directions
1. Stir fry your beef and chili powder in veggie oil until the beef is fully d1 then add the bean paste and stir.
2. Now add in the water and get everything boiling before adding in some pepper and salt.
3. Once the mix is boiling add in your tofu and cook the contents for 4 mins.
4. Shut the heat and crack your egg into the soup.
5. Stir everything and let the egg poach before adding a garnishing of green onions and sesame seeds.
6. Enjoy.

Korean
Curry

🥣 Prep Time: 20 mins

🕐 Total Time: 1 hr 10 mins

Servings per Recipe: 6
Calories	303 kcal
Fat	13.6 g
Carbohydrates	27.9g
Protein	17.6 g
Cholesterol	36 mg
Sodium	60 mg

Ingredients

1/4 C. olive oil, divided
1 1/2 lbs boneless chicken breast, cut into cubes
1 large yellow onion, cut into cubes
2 large russet potatoes, peeled and cut into cubes
3 large carrots, peeled and cut into cubes
4 C. water
1 tbsp Korean-style curry powder (such as Assi(R) mild curry powder), or more to taste

Directions

1. Stir fry your chicken in 2 tbsps of olive oil for 8 mins or until fully done.
2. Then in another pot stir fry your carrots, potatoes, and onions in more olive oil for 8 mins.
3. Add the chicken to the veggies and add some water.
4. Place a lid on the pot and let the contents gently boil for 22 mins.
5. Shut the heat and add in your curry and stir everything until the spice is completely mixed in.
6. Now cook everything for 25 more mins until the sauce is thick.
7. Enjoy.

CHICKEN
Stew

🥄 Prep Time: 20 mins

🕐 Total Time: 1 h 5 mins

Servings per Recipe: 4

Calories	896 kcal
Fat	69.1 g
Carbohydrates	136.1g
Protein	33.4 g
Cholesterol	121 mg
Sodium	1111 mg

Ingredients

1 1/2 C. water
1/4 C. soy sauce
2 tbsps rice wine
2 tbsps Korean red chili pepper paste (gochujang)
2 tbsps Korean red chili pepper flakes (gochugaru)
1 tbsp honey
1 tbsp white sugar
1 pinch ground black pepper
3 lbs bone-in chicken pieces, trimmed of fat and cut into

small pieces
10 oz. potatoes, cut into large chunks
2 carrots, cut into large chunks
1/2 large onion, cut into large chunks
4 large garlic cloves, or more to taste
2 slices fresh ginger, or more to taste
2 scallions, cut into 2-inch lengths
1 tbsp sesame oil
1 tsp sesame seeds

Directions

1. Get the following boiling in a big pot: chicken, water, black pepper, soy sauce, sugar, wine, honey, pepper paste, and pepper flakes.
2. Once everything is boiling set the heat to low and place a lid on the pot.
3. Let the contents cook for 17 mins.
4. Add in: ginger, potatoes, garlic, carrots, and onions and cook the mix for 17 more mins.
5. Take off the lid and continue cooking for 12 more mins.
6. Now add in some sesame seeds, scallions, and sesame oil.
7. Enjoy.

Filipino
Oxtail Stew

Prep Time: 2 hr 20 mins
Total Time: 2 hr 35 mins

Servings per Recipe: 6

Calories	395 kcal
Carbohydrates	14.9 g
Cholesterol	125 mg
Fat	21 g
Fiber	6.6 g
Protein	40.1 g
Sodium	683 mg

Ingredients

1 1/2 pounds beef oxtail, cut into pieces
1 large onion, quartered
2 cloves garlic, chopped
1 tsp salt
1/2 tsp ground black pepper, or to taste
1 large eggplant, cut into 2-inch chunks
1/2 head bok choy, cut into 1-inch pieces

1/2 pound fresh green beans, trimmed and snapped into 2-inch pieces
1/4 cup peanut butter, or as needed to thicken sauce

Directions

1. Bring the mixture of oxtail pieces, pepper, garlic and salt to boil in water before cooking it for two hours over medium heat.
2. Now add eggplant, green beans and bok choy into this mixture before cooking it for another 20 minutes or until the vegetables you just added are tender.
3. Add a mixture of peanut butter and some broth into the stew just before you serve it.

SALMON
Stew
(Abalos Style)

Prep Time: 10 mins

Total Time: 25 mins

Servings per Recipe: 4

Calories	223 kcal
Carbohydrates	4.8 g
Cholesterol	45 mg
Fat	11 g
Fiber	0.9 g
Protein	24.9 g
Sodium	466 mg

Ingredients
1 tbsp olive oil
4 cloves garlic, minced
1 onion, diced
1 tomato, diced
1 (14.75 ounce) can pink salmon
2 1/2 cups water
bay leaf (optional)
salt and ground black pepper to taste
1 tsp fish sauce (optional)

Directions
1. Cook onion and garlic in hot oil for about 5 minutes before adding tomato and salmon into it.
2. Cook for another 3 minutes and then add water, fish sauce, bay leaf, salt and pepper.
3. Cover the skillet and cook for 20 minutes.
4. Serve.

22   Salmon Stew: (Abalos Style)

Picadillo Filipino (Hamburger Abalos Soup)

Prep Time: 20 mins
Total Time: 1 hr 5 mins

Servings per Recipe: 6
Calories	233 kcal
Carbohydrates	16.9 g
Cholesterol	46 mg
Fat	11.5 g
Fiber	2.4 g
Protein	15.4 g
Sodium	862 mg

Ingredients

1 tbsp cooking oil
1 onion, diced
4 cloves garlic, minced
1 large tomato, diced
1 pound ground beef
4 cups water
1 large potato, diced

2 tbsps beef bouillon
2 tbsps fish sauce
salt and pepper to taste

Directions

1. Cook onions and garlic in hot oil over medium heat until tender add tomatoes and cook for another 3 minutes.
2. Now add ground beef and cook for about 5 more minutes or until the color has turned brown.
3. Add potato, fish sauce, pepper, beef bouillon, water and some salt into the pan and cook at low heat for 30 minutes while stirring regularly.
4. Serve.

FISH
Sinigang (Tilapia)

Prep Time: 5 mins

Total Time: 15 mins

Servings per Recipe: 10
Calories	112 kcal
Carbohydrates	13.4 g
Cholesterol	21 mg
Fat	1 g
Fiber	2.1 g
Protein	13.1 g
Sodium	63 mg

Ingredients
1/2 pound tilapia fillets, cut into chunks
1 small head bok choy, chopped
2 medium tomatoes, cut into chunks
1 cup thinly sliced daikon radish
1/4 cup tamarind paste
3 cups water
2 dried red chile peppers(optional)

Directions
1. Combine tilapia, radish, tomatoes, mixture of tamarind paste and water, chili peppers and bok choy.
2. Bring the mixture to boil and cook for 5 minutes to get fish tender.
3. Serve in appropriate bowls.

Sinigang Na Baka (Beef Based Veggie Soup)

🥣 Prep Time: 15 mins
🕐 Total Time: 1 hr

Servings per Recipe: 6	
Calories	304 kcal
Carbohydrates	15 g
Cholesterol	51 mg
Fat	19.7 g
Fiber	4.5 g
Protein	17.8 g
Sodium	1405 mg

Ingredients

2 tbsps canola oil
1 large onion, chopped
2 cloves garlic, chopped
1 pound beef stew meat, cut into 1 inch cubes
1 quart water
2 large tomatoes, diced
1/2 pound fresh green beans, rinsed and trimmed

1/2 medium head bok choy, cut into 1 1/2 inch strips
1 head fresh broccoli, cut into bite size pieces
1 (1.41 ounce) package tamarind soup base

Directions

1. Cook onion and garlic in hot oil and then add beef to get it brown.
2. Now add some water and bring it to a boil.
3. Turn the heat down to medium and cook for 30 minutes.
4. Cook for another 10 minutes after adding tomatoes and green beans.
5. Now add tamarind soup mix, bok choy and some broccoli into the mix and cook for 10 more minutes to get everything tender.

FILIPINO
Chicken Stew

Prep Time: 25 mins

Total Time: 1 hr 15 mins

Servings per Recipe: 8

Calories	554 kcal
Carbohydrates	28.4 g
Cholesterol	57 mg
Fat	32.3 g
Fiber	11.7 g
Protein	28.4 g
Sodium	645 mg

Ingredients
2 tbsps sesame oil
2 pounds boneless chicken pieces, cut into strips
2 tbsps fresh lemon juice
2 tbsps soy sauce
2 (15 ounce) cans coconut milk
1/4 cup red curry paste
1/4 cup flour
2 red bell peppers, chopped
1 sweet onion, chopped

1 red onion, chopped
2 cloves garlic, minced
2 large potatoes, cubed
2 (8 ounce) cans sliced bamboo shoots, drained
2 (8 ounce) cans sliced water chestnuts, drained
2 (8 ounce) cans baby corn, drained
1 (12 ounce) can sliced mushrooms, drained
1/4 cup chopped cilantro

Directions
1. Cook chicken, lemon juice, and soy sauce in hot sesame oil over medium heat for 5 minutes and in a bowl mix flour, coconut milk and curry paste, and add this mixture to the pan.

2. Now put bell pepper, red onion, garlic, potatoes, bamboo shoots, water chestnuts, sweet onion and mushrooms into the pan and cook at low heat for 45 minutes before adding cilantro and removing it from heat.

3. Serve.

Tofu Soup

🥄 Prep Time: 30 mins
🕐 Total Time: 38 mins

Servings per Recipe: 6
Calories   99 kcal
Fat   5 g
Carbohydrates   4.5g
Protein   9.6 g
Cholesterol   43 mg
Sodium   896 mg

Ingredients

1 tbsp vegetable oil
2 cloves garlic, minced
1 (1/2 inch) piece fresh ginger root, minced
6 oz. raw small shrimp, shelled and deveined
1 quart chicken stock
8 oz. tofu, diced small
1/3 C. frozen peas, thawed

1 tsp salt
1/2 tsp black pepper
1 tbsp cornstarch

Directions

1. Stir fry your ginger and garlic until aromatic, in hot oil then add the shrimp.
2. Stir fry everything until the shrimp is fully done.
3. Remove the shrimp from the pan and add in the stock.
4. Get everything boiling then combine in: pepper, tofu, salt, and peas.
5. Set the heat to low and let the mix simmer.
6. Now add some water and cornstarch together then pour this mix into the simmering liquid.
7. Let everything continue to cook for 2 mins then add the shrimp back in and get it hot.
8. Enjoy.

YUAN'S
Favorite Soup

Prep Time: 15 mins
Total Time: 35 mins

Servings per Recipe: 4
Calories	431 kcal
Fat	34 g
Carbohydrates	7.1g
Protein	24.1 g
Cholesterol	130 mg
Sodium	991 mg

Ingredients
1 lb ground turkey
1 egg
1 tbsp cornstarch
2 tsps sesame oil
1 tbsp minced fresh ginger root
1/4 tsp monosodium glutamate (MSG) (optional)
1 tsp salt
2 green onions, diced and divided
1 tbsp vegetable oil

1 head napa cabbage, cored and cut into chunks
2 C. low-sodium chicken broth
2 C. water, or as needed
1 tbsp soy sauce
2 tsps sesame oil

Directions
1. Get a bowl, combine: half of the green onions, turkey, salt, eggs, MSG (optional), cornstarch, ginger, and 2 tsps sesame oil.
2. Work the mix with your hands then place everything to the side.
3. Now being to fry your cabbage in hot veggie oil for 4 mins then add the broth, soy sauce, and water.
4. Get everything boiling then set the heat to a medium level.
5. Grab your meat mix and use two spoons to shape the mix into small balls.
6. Add these balls to the boiling mix.
7. Continue adding your meat mix to the soup, in this manner, then place a lid on the pot when all the balls have been added to the mix.
8. Cook the balls for 12 mins then add some salt. When serving the dish add some sesame oil and green onions.
9. Enjoy.

Taiwanese Corn Soup

Prep Time: 5 mins
Total Time: 15 mins

Servings per Recipe: 4
Calories   121 kcal
Fat   1.9 g
Carbohydrates   24.1g
Protein   5 g
Cholesterol   48 mg
Sodium   409 mg

Ingredients

1 (15 oz.) can cream style corn
1 (14.5 oz.) can low-sodium chicken broth
1 egg, beaten
1 tbsp cornstarch
2 tbsps water

Directions

1. Get the following boiling in a large pot: broth and cream corn.
2. Get a bowl, combine: water and cornstarch.
3. Mix the contents until smooth then add the mix with the boiling broth.
4. Let the broth continue to cook for 4 mins then add the whisked eggs slowly.
5. Stir the soup while adding in your eggs.
6. Enjoy.

EASY
Egg and Pea Soup

🥄 Prep Time: 2 mins

🕐 Total Time: 15 mins

Servings per Recipe: 6	
Calories	35 kcal
Fat	1.9 g
Carbohydrates	2.5g
Protein	< 2.4 g
Cholesterol	31 mg
Sodium	639 mg

Ingredients
4 C. seasoned chicken broth
1/2 C. frozen green peas
1 egg, beaten

Directions
1. Get your peas and broth boiling. Then once the mix is boiling add in your whisked eggs gradually to form ribbons.
2. Then add in your green onions and serve.
3. Enjoy.

Asian Corn Soup Cream Style

🍲 Prep Time: 10 mins
🕐 Total Time: 50 mins

Servings per Recipe: 6
Calories	157 kcal
Fat	3.3 g
Carbohydrates	16.2g
Protein	16 g
Cholesterol	26 mg
Sodium	1052 mg

Ingredients

1/2 lb skinless, boneless chicken breast meat - finely diced
1 tbsp broth
1/4 tsp salt
2 egg whites
1 (14.75 oz.) can cream-style corn
4 C. chicken broth

2 tsps soy sauce
1/4 C. water
2 tbsps cornstarch
4 slices crisp cooked turkey bacon, crumbled

Directions

1. Get a bowl, combine: chicken, egg whites, broth, and salt.
2. Combine in the cream corn and continue mixing everything until it's smooth.
3. Now get the following boiling in a wok: soy sauce and chicken broth.
4. Combine in the chicken mix and get everything boiling again.
5. Now set the heat to low, and cook the soup for 5 mins while stirring.
6. Combine some cornstarch and water then pour this mix into your boiling soup and keep stirring everything for 3 more mins. Then add in your bacon and serve.
7. Enjoy.

BAMBOO
Rice Soup

Prep Time: 10 mins
Total Time: 25 mins

Servings per Recipe: 6
Calories	295 kcal
Fat	17 g
Carbohydrates	24g
Protein	10.6 g
Cholesterol	60 mg
Sodium	641 mg

Ingredients

3 oz. baby shrimp
3 oz. skinless, boneless chicken pieces cut into chunks
1 egg
4 tbsps cornstarch
4 C. vegetable oil for frying
3 C. chicken broth
1 oz. mushrooms, diced
2 tbsps diced water chestnuts
1/8 C. diced bamboo shoots

1/3 C. fresh green beans, cut into 1 inch pieces
1/2 tsp salt
1 tbsp sherry
2/3 C. uncooked white rice

Directions

1. Get a bowl, combine: cornstarch, shrimp, egg, and chicken.

2. Get 3 C. of oil hot in a frying pan then add the chicken mix.

3. Fry the mix for 1 min then remove the oils.

4. Now add everything to a large pot with: the green beans, broth, bamboo shoots, salt, mushrooms, sherry, and water chestnuts.

5. Get everything boiling, set the heat to low, and let the mix gently cook.

6. At the time same as the soup is simmering get 1 C. of oil hot and toast your rice in it until the kernels are browned.

7. Combine the rice with the soup and let the mix cook until the rice is tender.

8. Enjoy.

Potato Soup

Prep Time: 10 mins
Total Time: 1 hr 55 mins

Servings per Recipe: 3
Calories   255 kcal
Fat   2.8 g
Carbohydrates   47.2g
Protein   11.6 g
Cholesterol   19 mg
Sodium   77 mg

Ingredients
3 potatoes, cubed
1 carrot, diced
1 turnip, diced
1 onion, diced
5 cloves garlic, minced
1 chicken leg
salt and pepper to taste

Directions
1. Get the following boiling: water, potatoes, chicken, carrots, garlic, turnips, and onions.
2. Once the mix is boiling, set the heat to a low level.
3. Cook the mix for 50 mins then add some pepper and salt.
4. Take out the chicken legs and remove their meat, once the chicken is cool enough to handle.
5. Place the meat back into the soup. Throw away the bones and skin.
6. Continue cooking the soup for 35 more mins.
7. Enjoy.

SUAN
La Dofu Tang (Tofu Soup)

🥄 Prep Time: 15 mins

🕐 Total Time: 25 mins

Servings per Recipe: 2

Calories	256 kcal
Fat	8.3 g
Carbohydrates	25.5g
Protein	21.2 g
Cholesterol	93 mg
Sodium	2390 mg

Ingredients
4 C. vegetable broth
1 (12 oz.) package silken tofu, diced
2 green onions, diced
1 eggs, beaten
1 portobello mushroom, halved and sliced
2 C. diced cabbage
1 tbsp Thai chile sauce
1 tbsp rice vinegar
3 tbsps soy sauce

1 tsp citric acid powder (optional)

Directions
1. Get your broth boiling then add the green onions and tofu.
2. Gradually pour in the whisked eggs to form long ribbons. Then combine in the cabbage and mushrooms.
3. Let the contents cook for 7 mins then shut the heat.
4. Add in your soy sauce, citric acid, vinegar, and chili sauce.
5. Enjoy.

Hot and Spicy Soup

🥣 Prep Time: 30 mins

🕐 Total Time: 1 hr

Servings per Recipe: 3

Calories	116 kcal
Fat	6.3 g
Carbohydrates	8.7g
Protein	7.4 g
Cholesterol	41 mg
Sodium	465 mg

Ingredients

5 dried wood ear mushrooms
4 dried shiitake mushrooms
8 dried tiger lily buds
4 C. chicken stock
1/3 C. diced bamboo shoots
1/3 C. lean ground turkey
1 tsp soy sauce
1/2 tsp white sugar
1 tsp salt

1/2 tsp ground white pepper
2 tbsps red wine vinegar
2 tbsps cornstarch
3 tbsps water
1/2 (16 oz.) package firm tofu, cubed
1 egg, lightly beaten
1 tsp sesame oil
2 tbsps thinly sliced green onion

Directions

1. In warm water, for 30 mins, submerge your tiger lily and mushrooms, in a bowl.
2. Now remove any stems and cut the mushrooms and tiger lilly.
3. Now get the following boiling in a large pot: turkey, mushrooms, bamboo shoots, tiger lily, and stock.
4. Let the mix cook for 12 mins then add: vinegar, soy sauce, white pepper, sugar, and salt.
5. Grab a small bowl, combine: some of the hot soup, 3 tbsps water, and cornstarch.
6. Mix everything until it's smooth then combine everything together and stir.
7. Get the mix completely boiling then add in the bean curds and cook the soup for 3 more mins.
8. Now shut the heat and slowly add in the eggs.
9. Let the eggs set then add the sesame oil and the scallions.
10. Enjoy.

CHI TAN T'ANG
(Classical Egg Drop Soup)

🥣 Prep Time: 10 mins

🕐 Total Time: 20 mins

Servings per Recipe: 6	
Calories	62 kcal
Fat	2.8 g
Carbohydrates	4.7g
Protein	4.5 g
Cholesterol	94 mg
Sodium	1872 mg

Ingredients
8 cubes chicken bouillon
6 C. hot water
2 tbsps cornstarch
2 tbsps soy sauce
3 tbsps distilled white vinegar
1 green onion, minced
3 eggs, beaten

Directions
1. Get a large pot and begin to heat some hot water and bouillon.
2. Stir and heat the mix until the bouillon is completely dissolved.
3. Now add in: the green onions, soy sauce, and vinegar.
4. Get the mix boiling then set the heat to low.
5. Slowly add in your whisked eggs while stirring.
6. Once the eggs have set, shut the heat.
7. Enjoy.

Cabbage Soup

Prep Time: 10 mins
Total Time: 50 mins

Servings per Recipe: 4
Calories	256 kcal
Fat	8.9 g
Carbohydrates	28g
Protein	17.9 g
Cholesterol	18 mg
Sodium	1623 mg

Ingredients

1 1/2 tbsps vegetable oil
1/4 small head cabbage, shredded
4 oz. lean chicken tenderloin, cut into thin strips
6 C. chicken broth
2 tbsps soy sauce
1/2 tsp minced fresh ginger root
8 fresh green onions, diced

4 oz. dry Chinese noodles

Directions

1. Stir fry your chicken and cabbage for 7 mins until the chicken is fully done.

2. Pour in the broth and add: ginger and soy sauce.

3. Stir the mix then get everything boiling.

4. Once the mix is boiling set the heat to low and let the mix cook for 12 mins.

5. Stir the contents at least 3 times.

6. Now add the noodles and onions and cook everything for 5 more mins.

7. Enjoy.

SWEET AND SPICY
Tofu Soup

Prep Time: 20 mins
Total Time: 50 mins

Servings per Recipe: 4

Calories	211 kcal
Fat	12 g
Carbohydrates	17.3g
Protein	11.3 g
Cholesterol	0 mg
Sodium	243 mg

Ingredients

1 tbsp vegetable oil
1 red bell pepper, diced
3 green onions, diced
2 C. water
2 C. chicken broth
1 tbsp soy sauce
1 tbsp red wine vinegar
1/4 tsp crushed red pepper flakes
1/8 tsp ground black pepper

1 tbsp cornstarch
3 tbsps water
1 tbsp sesame oil
6 oz. frozen snow peas
1 (8 oz.) package firm tofu, cubed
1 (8 oz.) can sliced water chestnuts, drained

Directions

1. Stir fry your green onions and bell peppers in oil for 7 mins then combine in: soy sauce, broth, and 2 C. of water.

2. Now set the heat to medium and let the mix cook for 7 more mins.

3. Get a bowl, combine: sesame oil, vinegar, 3 tbsps water, pepper flakes, cornstarch, and black pepper.

4. Stir the mix until it is smooth then pour it into the simmering broth.

5. Continue simmering the broth for 7 more mins until it gets thick then add in: water chestnuts, snow peas, and tofu.

6. Let the tofu cook for 12 mins.

7. Enjoy.

Easy
Wonton Soup

🥣 Prep Time: 5 mins
🕐 Total Time: 15 mins

Servings per Recipe: 4
Calories   293 kcal
Fat   9 g
Carbohydrates   33.5g
Protein   17.7 g
Cholesterol   84 mg
Sodium   3373 mg

Ingredients
8 C. chicken broth
3 tbsps soy sauce
2 tsps sesame oil
2 tsps rice wine vinegar
2 tsps lemon juice
2 tsps minced garlic
1 1/2 tsps chile-garlic sauce (such as Sriracha(R))

salt to taste
8 C. water
20 wontons

Directions
1. Get the following simmering: salt, broth, chili garlic sauce, sesame oil, garlic, wine vinegar, and lemon juice.
2. Let the mix gently simmer for 12 mins.
3. At the same time being to get some water boiling in another pot. Add the wontons to the boiling water and let the mix cook for 7 mins. Then combine the wontons to the simmering mix.
4. Enjoy.

ALTERNATIVE
Egg Drop Soup

Prep Time: 10 mins

Total Time: 20 mins

Servings per Recipe: 4
Calories	36 kcal
Fat	1.6 g
Carbohydrates	4g
Protein	1.7 g
Cholesterol	46 mg
Sodium	164 mg

Ingredients
1 egg
1/4 tsp salt
2 tbsps tapioca flour
1/4 C. cold water
4 C. chicken broth
1/8 tsp ground ginger
1/8 tsp minced fresh garlic
2 tbsps diced green onion
1/4 tsp Asian (toasted) sesame oil (optional)

1 pinch white pepper (optional)

Directions
1. Get a bowl and whisk your eggs with salt in it.
2. Get a 2nd bowl, mix: cold water and tapioca flour. Mix everything until its smooth.
3. Now get your garlic, ginger, and broth boiling.
4. Once the mix has boiled for about 2 mins add the tapioca mix and continue boiling everything for about 2 more mins until the mix is no longer cloudy and thick.
5. Remove the mix from the heat and add the eggs in gradually.
6. Combine the eggs in slowly in the form of a circle but do not stir the mix too much.
7. Once the eggs have set add a garnishing of white pepper, sesame oil, and onions.
8. Enjoy.

Chinese
Melon Soup

🥣 Prep Time: 30 mins

🕐 Total Time: 50 mins

Servings per Recipe: 10

Calories	173 kcal
Fat	10.8 g
Carbohydrates	9.4g
Protein	9.8 g
Cholesterol	70 mg
Sodium	1111 mg

Ingredients

1 lb ground turkey
2 tbsps cornstarch
1/2 bunch cilantro leaves, finely diced
3 tbsps soy sauce
2 tbsps white sugar
2 tbsps minced garlic
2 tbsps minced fresh ginger

2 eggs
6 C. water
2 lbs Chinese winter melon (dong gua), cut into
1 inch cubes
3 slices fresh ginger
1 tbsp salt
1 tbsp white sugar

Directions

1. Top your turkey with the following: ginger, cornstarch, garlic, cilantro, sugar, and soy sauce.
2. Add in the eggs and mix everything until it becomes slightly sticky.
3. Now add the following to a large pot: sugar, water, salt, winter melon, and ginger.
4. Get the mix boiling then set the heat to medium-low and cook everything for 7 mins.
5. At the same time being to form small balls from your turkey mix with a tsp.
6. Add the balls to the boiling mix.
7. Once you have added all the meat to the boiling mix let everything cook for 12 mins.
8. Enjoy.

NATURAL
Ramen Noodles

Prep Time: 10 mins

Total Time: 20 mins

Servings per Recipe: 4

Calories	280 kcal
Carbohydrates	53.6 g
Cholesterol	0 mg
Fat	4.4 g
Fiber	1.3 g
Protein	10.4 g
Sodium	1351 mg

Ingredients
4 cups vegetable broth
4 cups water
1 tbsp soy sauce
1 tbsp sesame oil
1 tbsp ground ginger
1 tbsp Sriracha hot sauce
9 ounces soba noodles

Directions
1. Bring everything except noodles to boil before adding noodles and cooking it for about seven minutes or until you see that they are tender.
2. Take noodles out into bowls and top with broth according to your choice.

New
Classical Ramen

Prep Time: 5 mins
Total Time: 15 mins

Servings per Recipe: 1
Calories	500 kcal
Carbohydrates	66 g
Cholesterol	191 mg
Fat	19.2 g
Fiber	4.5 g
Protein	17.4 g
Sodium	1796 mg

Ingredients
2 1/2 cups water
1 carrot, sliced
4 fresh mushrooms, sliced
1 (3 ounce) package ramen noodle pasta with flavor
packet
1 egg, lightly beaten
1/4 cup milk (optional)

Directions
1. Cook carrots and mushrooms in boiling water for about seven minutes before adding noodles and flavoring packets, and cooking all this for three more minutes.
2. Pour egg into the mixture very slowly, while stirring continuously for thirty seconds to get the egg cooked.
3. Add some milk before serving.

RAMEN
Re-Imagined

Prep Time: 5 mins

Total Time: 15 mins

Servings per Recipe: 2

Calories	291 kcal
Carbohydrates	42.4 g
Cholesterol	0 mg
Fat	10.2 g
Fiber	2.2 g
Protein	6.9 g
Sodium	1675 mg

Ingredients
3 1/2 cups vegetable broth
1 (3.5 ounce) package ramen noodles with dried vegetables
2 tsps soy sauce
1/2 tsp chili oil
1/2 tsp minced fresh ginger root
2 green onions, sliced

Directions
1. Bring a mixture of noodles and broth to boil over high heat before turning down the heat to medium and adding soy sauce, ginger and chili oil.
2. Cook this for about 10 minutes before adding sesame oil.
3. Garnish this with green onions before serving.

Super Easy
Coconut Soup Thai-Style

🥣 Prep Time: 25 mins
🕐 Total Time: 40 mins

Servings per Recipe: 8
Calories	314 kcal
Carbohydrates	17.2 g
Cholesterol	86 mg
Fat	21.6 g
Fiber	2.1 g
Protein	15.3 g
Sodium	523 mg

Ingredients
1 pound medium shrimp - peeled and deveined
2 (13.5 ounce) cans canned coconut milk
2 cups water
1 (1 inch) piece galangal, thinly sliced
4 stalks lemon grass, bruised and chopped
10 kaffir lime leaves, torn in half
1 pound shiitake mushrooms, sliced

1/4 cup lime juice
3 tbsps fish sauce
1/4 cup brown sugar
1 tsp curry powder
1 tbsp green onion, thinly sliced
1 tsp dried red pepper flakes

Directions
1. Cook shrimp in boiling water until tender.
2. Put coconut milk, water, lime leaves, galangal and lemon grass in a large sized pan and heat it up for about 10 minutes before transferring the coconut milk into a new pan, while discarding all the spices.
3. Heat up shiitake mushrooms in the coconut milk for five minutes before adding lime juice, curry powder, brown sugar and fish sauce into it.
4. When you want to serve it, heat up the shrimp in this soup for some time before pouring this into serving bowls.

A UNIQUELY SIMPLE
Cumber Soup
with Thai Roots

Prep Time: 15 mins

Total Time: 45 mins

Servings per Recipe: 4

Calories	67 kcal
Carbohydrates	6.8 g
Cholesterol	3 mg
Fat	4 g
Fiber	1.4 g
Protein	1.7 g
Sodium	702 mg

Ingredients
1 tbsp vegetable oil
3 cucumbers, peeled and diced
1/2 cup chopped green onion
2 1/2 cups chicken broth
1 1/2 tbsps lemon juice
1 tsp white sugar
salt and ground black pepper to taste

Directions
1. Cook cucumber in hot olive oil for about 5 minutes before adding green onions and cooking for another five minutes.
2. Add chicken broth, sugar and lemon juice into it before bringing all this to boil.
3. Turn down the heat to low and cook for another 20 minutes before adding salt and black pepper according to your taste.
4. Serve.

Charong's Favorite
Thai Soup of Ginger

Prep Time: 15 mins
Total Time: 25 mins

Servings per Recipe: 4	
Calories	415 kcal
Carbohydrates	7.3 g
Cholesterol	29 mg
Fat	39 g
Fiber	2.1 g
Protein	14.4 g
Sodium	598 mg

Ingredients
3 cups coconut milk
2 cups water
1/2 pound skinless, boneless chicken breast halves - cut into thin strips
3 tbsps minced fresh ginger root
2 tbsps fish sauce, or to taste
1/4 cup fresh lime juice

2 tbsps sliced green onions
1 tbsp chopped fresh cilantro

Directions
1. Bring the mixture of coconut milk and water to boil before adding chicken strips, and cooking it for three minutes on medium heat or until you see that the chicken is cooked through.
2. Now add ginger, green onions, lime juice, cilantro and fish sauce into it.
3. Mix it well and serve.

A THAI SOUP
of Veggies

Prep Time: 15 mins

Total Time: 50 mins

Servings per Recipe: 5

Calories	310 kcal
Carbohydrates	22.9 g
Cholesterol	55 mg
Fat	22.4 g
Fiber	5.7 g
Protein	8.5 g
Sodium	147 mg

Ingredients

1/4 cup butter
6 tomatoes, peeled and quartered
3 zucchini, cut into chunks
1 yellow onion, cut in half and quartered
1 red bell pepper, chopped
3 cloves garlic, roughly chopped
1/4 cup chopped fresh cilantro leaves
1 tbsp chopped fresh basil (preferably Thai basil)
1 tbsp lime juice

1 pinch salt
2 1/2 cups milk
3 tbsps coconut butter
1 tbsp curry powder
1/4 tsp ground turmeric
1/4 tsp ground ginger
1/8 tsp ground cumin
1 bay leaf
5 tbsps heavy whipping cream (optional)

Directions

1. Cook tomatoes, zucchini, onion, garlic, cilantro, red bell pepper, basil, lime juice, and salt in hot butter for about 25 minutes before transferring it to a blender and blending it until the required smoothness is achieved.

2. Cook milk, curry powder, turmeric, ginger, coconut butter, cumin, and bay leaf in the same pan for about 5 minutes or until you see that coconut butter has melted.

3. At the very end, add blended vegetables into it and cook for five more minutes.

4. Garnish with heavy cream before serving.

Easy
Coconut Soup

🥣 Prep Time: 35 mins

🕐 Total Time: 1 hr 5 mins

Servings per Recipe: 8
Calories	375 kcal
Fat	33.2 g
Carbohydrates	9.4g
Protein	13.7 g
Cholesterol	89 mg
Sodium	1059 mg

Ingredients
1 tbsp vegetable oil
2 tbsps grated fresh ginger
1 stalk lemon grass, minced
2 tsps red curry paste
4 C. chicken broth
3 tbsps fish sauce
1 tbsp light brown sugar

3 (13.5 oz.) cans coconut milk
1/2 lb fresh shiitake mushrooms, sliced
1 lb medium shrimp - peeled and deveined
2 tbsps fresh lime juice
salt to taste
1/4 C. chopped fresh cilantro

Directions
1. Stir fry your curry paste, lemongrass, and ginger in oil for 2 mins then add in the broth while continuing to stir everything.
2. Add in the brown sugar and fish sauce and let the contents gently boil for 17 mins.
3. Now add the mushrooms and the coconut milk.
4. Continue cooking everything for 7 more min.
5. Then combine in the shrimp and let the fish cook for 7 mins until it is fully done.
6. Now add some cilantro, salt, and lime juice.
7. Enjoy.

SPICY
Kale and Onion Soup

🥣 Prep Time: 15 mins

🕐 Total Time: 1 hr 15 mins

Servings per Recipe: 5
Calories	271 kcal
Fat	21.7 g
Cholesterol	72 mg
Sodium	1216 mg
Carbohydrates	6.8 g
Fiber	1.3 g
Protein	12.4 g

Ingredients

12 links spicy beef sausage, sliced
1 tbsp vegetable oil
3/4 C. minced onion
1 1/4 tsps minced garlic
2 tbsps chicken soup base
4 C. water
2 potatoes, halved and sliced
2 C. sliced kale
1/3 C. heavy cream

Directions

1. Set your oven at 300 degrees F before doing anything else.
2. Bake sausage links in the preheated oven for about 25 minutes before slicing it into half inch slices.
3. Cook onion and garlic in hot oil for one minute before adding broth, water, potatoes and cooking it for 14 minutes.
4. Turn down the heat to low and stir in sausage, kale and cream.
5. Cook for a few more minutes and serve.

Lemony
Soy Sauce Soup

Prep Time: 15 mins
Total Time: 50 mins

Servings per Recipe: 6
Calories	201 kcal
Fat	13.5 g
Carbohydrates	14.8g
Protein	7.5 g
Cholesterol	32 mg
Sodium	829 mg

Ingredients
4 tbsps unsalted butter
2 C. diced onions
1 lb fresh mushrooms, sliced
2 tsps dried dill weed
1 tbsp paprika
1 tbsp soy sauce
2 C. chicken broth

1 C. milk
3 tbsps all-purpose flour
1 tsp salt
ground black pepper to taste
2 tsps lemon juice
1/4 C. diced fresh parsley
1/2 C. sour cream

Directions
1. Stir fry your onions in butter for 6 mins. Then add in: broth, dill, soy sauce, and paprika. Place a lid on the pot once everything is boiling, then set the heat to low and cook for 17 mins.
2. Get a bowl, mix: flour and milk.
3. Add the flour mix to the broth pot. Then continue simmering for 15 more mins.
4. Season the soup with: sour cream, pepper, parsley, salt, and lemon juice.
5. Continue cooking for 6 more mins.
6. Enjoy.

JAPANESE
Mushroom Soup I (Shiitake, Beef, and Cheddar)

🥄 Prep Time: 10 mins
🕐 Total Time: 45 mins

Servings per Recipe: 8
Calories   163 kcal
Fat   11.4 g
Carbohydrates   5.1g
Protein   8.7 g
Cholesterol   24 mg
Sodium   809 mg

Ingredients
4 slices turkey bacon, diced
1/2 white onion, diced
1 lb shiitake mushrooms, sliced
2 cloves garlic, diced
black pepper to taste
2 leaves fresh sage, diced
6 C. beef broth
1 C. shredded Cheddar cheese

Directions
1. Fry your bacon in a big pan for 7 mins. Add in your onions and then fry for another 6 mins.
2. Now add: sage, mushrooms, pepper, and garlic. Cook this mix for 12 more mins.
3. Add the broth and get everything lightly boiling. Let the contents simmer for 10 mins with a low level of heat.
4. Finally before everything is done add in your cheese and let it melt.
5. Enjoy hot.

Japanese

Mushroom Soup II (Shiitake, Miso, and Tofu)

Prep Time: 10 mins
Total Time: 20 mins

Servings per Recipe: 4
Calories   92 kcal
Fat   2.5 g
Carbohydrates   11.8g
Protein   5.5 g
Cholesterol   0 mg
Sodium   1406 mg

Ingredients

4 C. vegetable broth
4 shiitake mushrooms, thinly sliced
1/4 C. miso paste
4 tsps soy sauce
1/3 C. diced firm tofu
2 green onions, trimmed and thinly sliced

Directions

1. Get a bowl, mix: soy sauce, and miso paste
2. Boil your broth in a big pot and then combine in your mushrooms and set the heat to its lowest level.
3. Let the mushrooms lightly boil for 5 mins.
4. Now add the soy sauce mix as well as the tofu and let the contents continue to boil for 3 more mins.
5. Place your soup in serving bowls and then top with onions.
6. Enjoy.

ENJOY THE RECIPES?
KEEP ON COOKING
WITH 6 MORE FREE COOKBOOKS!

EASY SAMOSA COOKBOOK

A KITCHEN IN MOROCCO
CLASSICAL MOROCCAN RECIPES

THE BIRYANI BASH
A COLLECTION OF THE MOST UNIQUE BIRYANI RECIPES
UMM MARYAM

EASY BEANS COOKBOOK
A COLLECTION OF SIMPLE AND UNIQUE RECIPES

EASY SUSHI COOKBOOK
CHEF MAGGIE CHOW

EASY DUMP DINNER COOKBOOK
CHEF MAGGIE CHOW

Click the link below and simply enter your email address to join the club and receive your 6 cookbooks.

http://booksumo.com/magnet

Printed in Poland
by Amazon Fulfillment
Poland Sp. z o.o., Wrocław